Pupil Book 4

Spelling

Skills

Authors: Sarah Snashall and Chris Whitney

William Collins' dream of knowledge for all began with the publication of his first book in 1819.

A self-educated mill worker, he not only enriched millions of lives, but also founded a flourishing publishing house. Today, staying true to this spirit, Collins books are packed with inspiration, innovation and practical expertise. They place you at the centre of a world of possibility and give you exactly what you need to explore it.

Collins. Freedom to teach.

Published by Collins
An imprint of HarperCollins*Publishers*
The News Building
1 London Bridge Street
London
SE1 9GF

Publishing Director: Lee Newman
Publishing Manager: Helen Doran
Senior Editor: Hannah Dove
Project Manager: Emily Hooton
Authors: Sarah Snashall and Chris Whitney
Development Editor: Jessica Marshall
Copy-editor: Karen Williams
Proofreaders: Tracy Thomas and Ros Davies
Cover design and artwork: Amparo Barrera and Ken Vail Graphic Design
Internal design concept: Amparo Barrera
Typesetter: Jouve India Private Ltd
Illustrations: Aptara and QBS
Production Controller: Rachel Weaver

Printed and bound by Grafica Veneta S.p.A.

Browse the complete Collins catalogue at
www.collins.co.uk

MIX
Paper from
responsible sources
FSC™ C007454
FSC
www.fsc.org

FSC™ is a non-profit international organisation established to promote the responsible management of the world's forests. Products carrying the FSC label are independently certified to assure consumers that they come from forests that are managed to meet the social, economic and ecological needs of present and future generations, and other controlled sources.

Find out more about HarperCollins and the environment at
www.harpercollins.co.uk/green

Contents

Adding suffixes beginning with vowels to words of more than one syllable

A suffix is a group of letters added to the end of a root word. When you add a suffix starting with a vowel to a word of more than one syllable, the spelling rule depends on whether the last syllable is stressed or not. If the last syllable is stressed, double the final consonant. For example: **gar**den + –**er** = gardener, but be**gin** + –**er** = begi**nn**er.

If a root word ends in **l**, the last letter is doubled whatever the syllable stress.

Get started

Copy and complete the table by sorting these words into two groups: words where the final consonant is doubled when a suffix is added and words where it is not. One has been done for you.

1. garden
2. listen
3. water
4. begin
5. prefer
6. forget
7. answer

Consonant not doubled with suffix	Consonant doubled with suffix
garden	

Try these

Copy and complete the table by adding suffixes to these words. One has been done for you.

Root word	–ed	–ing
wonder	wondered	
regret		
prefer		
offer		

Now try these

Add **–er**, **–ed** or **–ing** to each of these words and then use them in sentences of your own. An example has been done for you.

1. enrol
2. forbid
3. target
4. limit
5. commit
6. cancel
7. admit
8. visit

Answer: Jack wished he had <u>enrolled</u> for swimming lessons.

The /i/ sound spelt y

Remember, there are some words in which the **/i/** sound is spelt as a letter **y**. For example, the **y** in g**y**m stands for the same sound as the **i** in r**i**m. Here are some other words that follow this pattern: m**y**th, p**y**ramid, m**y**stery.

Get started

Copy and complete the words by adding the missing letter, **i** or **y**. One has been done for you.

1. p_ramid

   Answer: *pyramid*

2. s_lly

3. g_m

4. cr_stal

5. s_mptom

6. pr_nce

7. m_stery

8. thr_lling

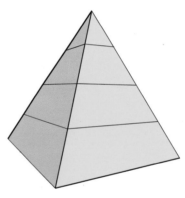

Try these

Read these sentences. Decide if the underlined word is spelt correctly or not. Write 'correct' or 'incorrect'. If the word is spelt wrong, write the correct spelling.

1. Nayati enjoyed visiting the <u>piramids</u> and would remember them forever.

   Answer: *incorrect – pyramids*

2. The photos were amazing – now I want to go to <u>Egipt</u> too!

3. This rainy weather is <u>tipical</u> in winter!

4. The music club's <u>simbol</u> is a violin.

5. My Uncle Jim tells some very <u>misterious</u> stories!

6. The fluffy young <u>cignets</u> will turn into elegant swans.

7. Frankie had learned the <u>lirics</u> to his favourite song.

8. The <u>gimnast</u> did a flip and landed on her feet.

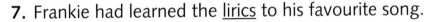

Now try these

Correct the spellings of these words and use them in sentences of your own. One has been done for you.

1. rhithm

   Answer: *Claire loves to play exciting <u>rhythms</u> on the drums.*

2. sillable   3. phisical   4. cimbal   5. histerical

6. sistem   7. oxigen   8. liric

The /u/ sound spelt ou

In some words, the letters **ou** are pronounced as if they were a **u**. For example, the **ou** in t**ou**ch stands for the same sound as the **u** in m**u**ch.

Get started

Check the spelling of the underlined word in each sentence. If the spelling is right, write 'correct'. If the spelling is wrong, write 'incorrect' and then write the correct spelling of the word. One has been done for you.

1. Chrissie needed <u>courage</u> to go and see the dentist.

   Answer: *correct*

2. I have always been good friends with my <u>cusin</u>.

3. Cary waved the brush and finished his painting with a <u>flourish</u>.

4. Tariq plays the <u>troumpet</u> in the school band.

5. Bea <u>jumped</u> over the puddle.

6. Miss Freeman said Louis was looking very <u>scruffy</u>.

7. Lia borrowed Katka's <u>hairbroush</u> without asking.

8. That maths test was really <u>tugh</u>.

Try these

Copy these sentences and correct the incorrectly spelt words. One has been done for you.

1. Grandad hasn't planted enugh tomatoes.

   Answer: *Grandad hasn't planted <u>enough</u> tomatoes.*

2. Are you sure you have enugh time to clean up before Mum comes back?

3. Mr Godwin always encurages us to enjoy science.

4. Rajesh saw a cuple of robins nesting in the tree.

5. Kerry has a lot of truble learning her spellings.

6. It's tugh work climbing hills!

7. Zahra's cookery teacher said it was important to be well nurished.

8. You can look at the paintings but you can't tuch them.

Now try these

Correct the spelling of these words and use them in sentences of your own. One has been done for you.

1. flurish

   Answer: *Katja finished her painting with a <u>flourish</u>.*

2. cuple   3. nurish   4. curage

5. cusin   6. duble

7. rugh   8. enugh

9

The prefixes dis– and mis–

A prefix is a group of letters that you can add to the start of a root word. The prefix **dis–** normally means 'not'. For example: **dis–** + agree = **dis**agree

The prefix **mis–** normally means 'badly' or 'incorrectly'. For example: **mis–** + spell = **mis**spell

Sometimes we use the prefixes **dis–** and **mis–** when there is not a clear root word.

Get started

Look at these pairs of words. Copy out the word from each pair that has the correct prefix. One has been done for you.

1. mismatched / dismatched

   Answer: *mismatched*

2. misagree / disagree

3. misspell / disspell

4. misshape / disshape

5. miscourage / discourage

6. misobey / disobey

7. misbehave / disbehave

8. misgraceful / disgraceful

Try these

Add the correct prefix, **dis–** or **mis–**, to each of these root words and write the new word. One has been done for you.

1. ____conduct

   Answer: *misconduct*

2. ____honest

3. ____approval

4. ____guided

5. ____connect

6. ____judge

7. ____understand

8. ____like

Now try these

Add the correct prefix, **dis–** or **mis–**, to each word. Then use it in a sentence of your own. One has been done for you.

1. similar

   Answer: *Although they are twins, the girls' tastes are dissimilar.*

2. agree   3. matched

4. calculated   5. judge

6. satisfied   7. understood

8. loyal

The prefixes in-, ir-, im- and il-

The prefix **in–** is used to mean 'not'. When you add **in–** to a root word, you do not change the spelling of the root word. But sometimes you do have to change the spelling of **in–**.

If you add **in–** to a root word beginning with **r**, **in–** becomes **ir–**. For example: **ir**responsible

If you add **in–** to a root word beginning with **m** or **p**, **in–** becomes **im–**. For example: **im**possible

If you add **in–** to a root word beginning with **l**, **in–** becomes **il–**. For example: **il**logical

Get started

Copy the words below, separating the prefix and root word. One has been done for you.

1. irresistible

   Answer: *ir / resistible*

2. independent

3. indefinitely

4. irreplaceable

5. illegal

6. irregular

7. immortal

8. incorrect

Try these

Copy and complete the words by adding the correct prefix, **in–**, **ir–**, **im–** or **il–**. One has been done for you.

1. ____credible

    Answer: *incredible*

2. ____considerate

3. ____resistible

4. ____mobile

5. ____ability

6. ____literate

7. ____practical

8. ____describable

Now try these

Use the words below in
sentences of your own.
An example has been done for you.

improbable, immeasurable,
irreplaceable, independent,
inability, illegible, immobile,
inescapable

Answer: It is <u>improbable</u> that you will see a
monkey riding on a crocodile.

The prefixes re– and inter–

The prefix **re–** means 'again'. The prefix **inter–** means 'between' or 'among'. When you add **re–** or **inter–** to a word, you do not have to make any changes to the root word.

For example: **re**discover, **inter**national

Get started

Add the prefix **re–** or **inter–** to each word and write the new word. One has been done for you.

1. ____route

   Answer: *reroute*

2. ____departmental

3. ____interpret

4. ____call

5. ____consider

6. ____adjust

7. ____related

8. ____build

Try these

Copy each word and write a short definition for it. Use a dictionary if you need to. One has been done for you.

1. rewrite

   Answer: *to write something again*

2. react

3. readjust

4. redial

5. international

6. rearrange

7. interact

8. interchangeable

Now try these

Use the words below in sentences of your own. An example has been done for you.

reread, rewrap, rewind, relive, intermingle, intermission, intersection, interview

Answer: *Jacob has <u>reread</u> his favourite book five times.*

The prefixes sub– and super–

The prefix **sub–** means 'under' or 'less than'. The prefix **super–** means 'above' or 'more than'. When you add **sub–** or **super–** to a root word, you do not change the spelling of the root word.

For example: **sub**way, **super**visor

Get started

Write these words, splitting the word into its prefix and root word. One has been done for you.

1. supermarket

   Answer: super / market

2. subdivide

3. subsection

4. superheated

5. subordinate

6. subclass

7. superbug

8. supercharge

Try these

Add the prefix **sub–** or **super–** to these root words and write the new words. One has been done for you.

1. ____market

   Answer: *supermarket*

2. ____impose

3. ____marine

4. ____merge

5. ____standard

6. ____continent

7. ____tropical

8. ____heated

Now try these

Use the words below in sentences of your own. An example has been done for you.

subsection, supermarket, superstar, subheading, submarine, subcontract, submerge, superglue

Answer: *The Sunday newspaper had many different <u>subsections</u>.*

The prefixes anti– and auto–

The prefix **anti–** is used to mean 'against'. The prefix **auto–** is used to mean 'self' or 'own'.

For example: **anti**biotics, **auto**graph

Get started

Write these words, splitting each word into its prefix and root word. One has been done for you.

1. automobile

   Answer: *auto / mobile*

2. antioxidant

3. antiglare

4. antithesis

5. autograph

6. autopilot

7. autodidact

8. autotimer

Try these

Add the prefix **anti–** or **auto–** to these root words and write the new word. One has been done for you.

1. _____ septic

    Answer: *antiseptic*

2. _____ mobile

3. _____ biography

4. _____ dote

5. _____ matter

6. _____ bacterial

7. _____ viral

8. _____ body

Now try these

Use the words below in sentences of your own. An example has been done for you.

antiseptic, antidote, autopilot, automaton, anticlimax, autograph, antihero, antisocial

Answer: *Emma cleaned her graze with <u>antiseptic</u> lotion.*

Can you remember the spellings you've learned this term?
Carry out these activities to find out.

A. Correct the spelling of each word.

1. mith
2. occured
3. curageous
4. ilegal
5. sirup

6. enugh
7. mispell
8. inpossible
9. bicicle
10. cuple

B. Choose the correct spelling for each of these words.

1. forgotten / forgoten
2. curage / courage
3. glorius / glorious
4. interview / inteview
5. distaken / mistaken
6. transferring / transfering
7. autamatic / automatic
8. listened / listenned

C. Use the prefixes **dis–**, **mis–**, **ir–**, **im–**, **super–**, **sub–** or **auto–** with each word in bold to write a word that matches the meaning of each phrase.

1. not **patient**

2. not **honest**

3. **judge** wrongly

4. not **relevant**

5. a shop that is like a huge **market**

6. an ointment to stop wounds becoming **septic**

7. part of a **continent**

8. a **standard** below what is acceptable

The suffix −ation

The suffix **−ation** turns verbs into nouns.
For example: inform → inform**ation**

If the verb ends in an **e**, remove the **e** before
adding **−ation**.
For example: aspir**e** → aspir**ation**

Get started

Look at these nouns. Write the verb related to each noun.
One has been done for you.

1. alteration

   Answer:  alter

2. confrontation

3. temptation

4. condensation

5. accusation

6. sensation

7. preservation

8. reputation

Try these

Choose the correct spelling for each word. Then write the word. One has been done for you.

1. determination / determineation

   Answer: *determination*

2. compilation / compileation

3. reformtion / reformation

4. converseation / conversation

5. determination / determineation

6. infestation / infesteation

7. obligeation / obligation

8. coloniseation / colonisation

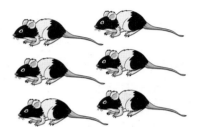

Now try these

Use these words in sentences of your own. An example has been done for you.

condensation, alteration, frustration, temptation, information, inclination

Answer: *The windows were wet from* <u>condensation</u>.

The suffix —ly

You can turn an adjective into an adverb by adding the suffix **–ly**.
For example: final + **–ly** = finally

However, if the root word has more than one syllable and ends in **y**, change the **y** to an **i**.
For example: pretty + **–ly** = prettily

If the root word ends with **le**, change the **le** to **–ly**.
For example: simple + **–ly** = simply

If the root word ends with **ic**, add **–ally** instead of **–ly**.
For example: basic + **–ally** = basically

A few words do not fit the rules. These have to be learned and remembered.
For example: **truly**, **wholly**

Get started

Copy the table below. Add the suffix **–ally** or **–ly** to the following words and copy them into the correct column of your table. One has been done for you.

1. comic
2. humble
3. able
4. historic
5. critic
6. scribble
7. logic
8. terrible

Words ending in –ally	Words ending in –ly
comically	

Try these

Change each adjective into an adverb by adding the correct suffix. One has been done for you.

1. energetic

    Answer: *energetically*

2. heroic

3. usual

4. happy

5. poetic

6. noble

7. greedy

Now try these

Use the following words in sentences of your own. An example has been done for you.

brightly, skilfully, sumptuously, happily, frantically, truly, wholly, realistically

Answer: *The sun shone <u>brightly</u>.*

The ending –sure

The buzzy **/zhur/** sound at the end of a word is always spelt **–sure** as in mea**sure**, trea**sure** and lei**sure**.

This sound is different from the **/sher/** sound at the end of blu**sher**, cru**sher** and pre**ssure**.

Can you hear the difference?

Get started

Copy the table. Find the correctly spelt words and write them in the first column of your table. Find the misspelt words and write them with the spellings corrected in the second column. One has been done for you.

1. pleasure

2. meazure

3. treasure

4. enclozure

5. closure

6. composhure

7. leisure

8. discomposuore

Correctly spelt words	Corrected words
pleasure	

Try these

Put the letters in the correct order to spell each word.
One has been done for you.

1. crmupoeos

   Answer: composure

2. eislersdpua

3. eatrresu

4. csloiuders

5. eulrsie

6. xesrpeuo

Now try these

Use these words in sentences of your own. An example has been done for you.

enclosure, displeasure, pleasure, composure, closure, exposure, treasure

Answer: The children looked at the chickens in their wire enclosure.

The endings –ture, –cher and –tcher

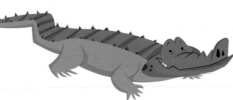

The /**cher**/ sound at the end of a word can be spelt:

–**ture** as in fu**ture** and pic**ture**
–**cher** as in tea**cher** and ri**cher**
–**tcher** as in ca**tcher** and stre**tcher**

Get started

Copy and complete the table to sort these words into two groups according to how the /**cher**/ sound is spelt: –**ture** or –**cher**/–**tcher**.

1. adventure
2. pasture
3. agriculture
4. richer
5. signature
6. gesture
7. catcher
8. departure

–ture	–cher/–tcher
adventure	

Try these

Choose from the two word endings and copy out the correct word. One has been done for you.

1. texture / texcher

   Answer: *texture*

2. architecture / architeccher

3. watcher / wature

4. leccher / lecture

5. pitcher / piture

6. feacher / feature

7. streture / stretcher

8. nurcher / nurture

Now try these

Use the words below in sentences of your own. An example has been done for you.

agriculture, departure, fracture, vulture, gesture, future, sculpture, puncture

Answer: <u>*Agriculture*</u> *is the science or practice of farming.*

The ending —sion

The buzzy **/zhun/** sound at the end of a word is always spelt **–sion** as in televi**sion**, divi**sion** and confu**sion**.

This sound is different from the **/shun/** sound at the end of man**sion**, comple**tion** and mis**sion**.

Can you hear the difference?

Get started

Find the spelling mistakes in each word and write the word correctly. One has been done for you.

1. revizion

    Answer: *revision*

2. illushun

3. excurtion

4. confuzhon

5. divizhun

6. verzion

7. televizion

8. averzion

30

Try these

Words with **–sion** at the end are nouns. Copy the two lists of words and match each noun to its related verb. One has been done for you.

Noun	Verb
conclusion	revise
television	conclude
erosion	divert
revision	explode
diversion	televise
explosion	invade
implosion	erode
invasion	implode

Now try these

Use these words in sentences of your own. An example has been done for you.

television, diversion, invasion, explosion, erosion, diversion, conclusion, occasion

Answer: *Aggie settled down to watch some television.*

The suffix —ous

Many adjectives end with the suffix —ous.

If the root word ends with e, drop the e before adding —ous, for example, fame → famous.

If the root word ends with a soft /g/ sound, keep the final e, for example, courage → courageous.

If the root word ends with y, change y to i before adding —ous, for example, vary → various.

If the root word ends with our, change our to or before adding the —ous, for example, glamour → glamorous.

Sometimes there is not a clear root word, for example, obvious.

If there is an /ee/ sound before the —ous, it is normally spelt with an i, for example, envious.

However, sometimes this /ee/ sound is spelt with an e, for example, spontaneous.

There are exceptions to these rules.

Get started

Identify and write the root word of each adjective. One has been done for you.

1. ridiculous   Answer: *ridicule*   2. humorous
3. miraculous   4. envious
5. vigorous   6. prosperous
7. hazardous   8. famous

Try these

Find the spelling mistakes in each word and write the word correctly. One has been done for you.

1. adventureous

   Answer: adventurous

2. spontanyous

3. spaceious

4. jealious

5. numarous

6. humourous

7. outragouse

8. mischievius

Now try these

Use these words in sentences of your own. An example has been done for you.

famous, nauseous, contagious, obvious, generous, momentous, mischievous, anonymous

Answer: Adjay's virus was <u>contagious</u>, so the doctor told him to stay in bed.

The endings –tion, –sion, –ssion and –cian

There are different ways of spelling the **/shun/** sound: **–tion**, **–ssion**, **–sion** and **–cian**.

The most common way of spelling the **/shun/** sound is **–tion**. Use this when the root word ends in **t** or **te**, for example, inje**ct** → inje**ction**. If the root word ends in **te** drop the final **e** before adding **–ion**, for example, comple**te** → comple**tion**.

For root words ending in **ss** or **mit**, spell the **/shun/** sound **–ssion**. For root words ending in **d** or a consonant then **se**, spell the **/shun/** sound **–sion**. If the root word ends in **d**, drop the **d** before adding **–sion**, for example, exten**d** → exten**sion**.

For root words ending in **c** or **s**, spell the **/shun/** sound **–cian**. If the root word ends in **cs**, drop the final **s** before adding **–ian**, for example, mathemati**cs** → mathemati**cian**.

Get started

Choose the suffix that makes the spelling correct for each word. Then write the correct word. One has been done for you.

1. temptation / temptassion / temptasion

   Answer: *temptation*

2. completion / complession / complecian

3. beautition / beautission / beautician

4. examinasion / examination / examinassion

5. tention / tenssion / tension

Try these

Add the **/shun/** endings to these root words and write them out. One has been done for you.

1. confess

Answer: *confession*

2. pollute

3. except

4. electric

5. admit

6. comprehend

7. mathematics

8. submit

Now try these

Use these words in sentences of your own. One has been done for you.

vacation, fiction, mission, immersion, expansion, fraction, obsession, musician

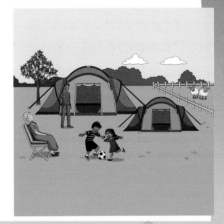

Answer: *This year we went camping for our <u>vacation</u>.*

The /k/ sound spelt ch

There are some words where the **/k/** sound is spelt **ch**. For example, the **ch** in monar**ch** is pronounced the same as the **k** in ban**k**er.

Get started

Copy and complete the table and sort these words into two groups: words where the **/k/** sound is spelt **ch** and words where it is not. One has been done for you.

1. monarch
2. skunk
3. anchor
4. chemistry
5. kite
6. character
7. cake
8. seek

The /k/ sound spelt ch	The /k/ sound not spelt ch
monarch	

Try these

Choose whether to fill in each gap with the letters **ch** or **c**.
Then write the word. One has been done for you.

1. __aos

    Answer: *chaos*

2. __ook

3. or__estra

4. S__otland

5. te__nology

6. e__o

7. s__ary

8. stoma__

Now try these

Correct the spellings of these words and use them in sentences
of your own. One has been done for you.

1. kord

    Answer: *Charlie strummed a*
    chord on her guitar.

2. kemist

3. kemistry

4. ankor

5. kaos

6. skeme

7. teknical

The /sh/ sound spelt ch

In most words, the **/sh/** sound is spelt with the letters **sh** as in **sh**ower.

However, in some words the **/sh/** sound is spelt with the letters **ch** as in **ch**ef.

Get started

Find the spelling mistake in each word and write the word correctly. One has been done for you.

1. shefs

Answer: *chefs*

2. shicane

3. shateau

4. quishe

5. shauffeur

6. croshet

7. sashet

8. shaperone

Try these

Put the letters in the correct order to spell each word.
One has been done for you.

1. hctue

   Answer: *chute*

2. ousmtache

3. nmaechi

4. echandlier

5. lcathe

6. acuratphe

7. uhicqe

8. eicnh

Now try these

Use these words in sentences of your own.
An example has been done for you.

machines, brochure, chandelier, parachute,
chauffeur, quiche, nonchalant, ricochet

Answer: *Computers are very useful machines.*

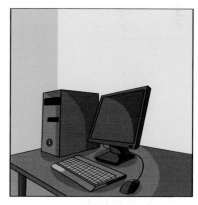

Review unit 2

Can you remember the spellings you've learned this term?
Carry out these activities to find out.

A. Choose the correct the spelling of each word.

1. sachet / sashet
2. mashine / machine
3. chorus / corus
4. pollution / pollusion
5. admition / admission
6. spacious / spacous

7. ridiculious / ridiculous
8. conclusion / conclussion
9. feature / featcher
10. meazure /measure
11. sensation / sensassion

B. Add the suffixes to the words. Remember, you might need to change the ending of the original word before you add the suffix.

1. accuse + –ation
2. oblige + –ation
3. prepare + –ation
4. terrible + –ly
5. crumble + –ly
6. crazy + –ly
7. humour + –ous
8. admit + **/shun/** sound

C. Complete and write down the missing word from each of these sentences.

1. The parents gave Timothy Jones a spon__ __ __ __ __ __ __ round of applause.

2. Ramah drew a smiley face in the conden__ __ __ __ __ __ on the window.

3. Thomas eyed the sticky doughnut gree__ __ __ __.

4. Mabel had a swimming party at the l__ __ __ __ __ __ centre.

5. We were exhausted after our muddy adven__ __ __ __ in the woods.

6. The magician didn't really cut Mrs Parker in half – it was just an ill__ __ __ __ __.

7. Mira__ __ __ __ __ __ly, everyone survived the plane crash.

8. Please ask your parents to sign the perm__ __ __ __ __ __ form.

9. The pirates pulled up the a__ __ __ __r and sailed away.

The /k/ sound spelt –que and the /g/ sound spelt –gue

In some words, the **/k/** sound is spelt –**que**, for example, barbe**que**.

In some words, the **/g/** sound is spelt –**gue**, for example, ro**gue**.

Get started

Find the spelling mistake in each word and write the word correctly. One has been done for you.

1. boutigue

   Answer: *boutique*

2. antigue

3. cataloque

4. vaque

5. fatique

6. grotesgue

7. tonque

8. merinque

Try these

Copy the sentences, adding a word from the box below to fill each gap. One has been done for you.

colleague	intrigue	opaque	plague	physique

1. My _____ was on holiday last week.

   Answer: My <u>colleague</u> was on holiday last week.

2. The athlete trained hard to keep his _____ in good shape.

3. The plot of his latest story was full of mystery and _____.

4. Many of the villagers were struck down with the _____ and died.

5. The windows in the room were made of _____ glass.

Now try these

Use these words in sentences of your own. An example has been done for you.

league, dialogue, intrigue, boutique, grotesque, rogue, colleague, opaque

Answer: One day, John and Casper hoped to play in the big <u>league</u>.

The /s/ sound spelt sc

There are several words in English where the **/s/** sound is spelt **sc**, for example, **sc**ent.

Get started

Each gap represents a **/s/** sound. Write the words, correctly filling the gaps with the letters **s** or **sc**. One has been done for you.

1. ca__es

   Answer: cases

2. __ene

3. de__end

4. lo__t

5. __enery

6. citru__

7. __ience

8. __ocial

Try these

Find the spelling mistakes in the words below and write each word correctly. Remember, /s/ can be spelt **s**, **c** or **sc**. One has been done for you.

1. seenic

Answer: *scenic*

2. cresent

3. desent

4. senscible

5. balanse

6. scolid

Now try these

Use these words in sentences of your own. An example has been done for you.

scissors, discipline, descend, adolescent, fascinate, ascend, scent

Answer: *Emily used the sharp* _*scissors*_ *to cut the paper shapes.*

The /ay/ sound spelt ei, eigh and ey

There are lots of different ways of spelling the **/ay/** sound including these three spelling patterns: **ei**, **eigh** and **ey**.

For example:

- v**ei**n
- w**eigh**
- conv**ey**

Get started

Write the letters in the correct order to spell each word. One has been done for you.

1. engih

   Answer: *neigh*

2. vonecy

3. geionruhb

4. eliv

5. byeo

6. ewgih

7. egry

8. tighe

Try these

Copy and complete the sentences by choosing the correct spelling of each word. One has been done for you.

1. Tracey chose _____ shoes for the party.
   (beigh / beige / beyge)

   Answer: *Tracey chose <u>beige</u> shoes for the party.*

2. The horses in the stable _____.
   (neyd / nejd / neighed)

3. The well-trained horse always _____ his master. (obeighed / obeid / obeyed)

4. There are many _____ in Lapland.
   (reighndeer / reindeer / reyndeer)

5. When it snows, I play on my _____. (sley / sleigh / slei)

6. Jack was learning to _____. (abseil / abseyl / abseighl)

7. We use birthday cards to _____ our greetings.
   (convei / conveigh / convey)

8. Her face was hidden by her bridal _____.
   (veil / veighl / veyl)

Now try these

Use these words in sentences of your own.
An example has been done for you.

neighbour, beige, survey, reign, veil, weigh, weightlifter

Answer: *Beth's <u>neighbour</u> Chris is really good at football.*

The possessive apostrophe with plural words

A possessive apostrophe shows that something belongs to a person or a thing.

If the person or thing is singular, add an apostrophe + **s**. For example: the girl**'s** bedroom = the bedroom of one girl.

If the person or thing is plural and ends in **s**, then just add an apostrophe. For example: the girls**'** bedroom = the bedroom of more than one girl.

If the plural form of the thing does not end with an **s**, add an apostrophe + **s**. For example: the children**'s** bedroom = the bedroom of the children.

If the singular form of the person or thing ends in **s**, add an apostrophe + **s**. For example: Louis**'s** bedroom = the bedroom of Louis; the class**'s** books = the books of the class.

Get started

Copy and complete the table and sort these words into singular (one) or plural (more than one). One has been done for you.

1. horses'   2. lion's

3. class's   4. actresses'

5. hero's   6. children's

Singular	Plural
	horses'

Try these

Copy each sentence, choosing the correct word to complete it. One has been done for you.

1. The _____ whistles were loud. (policemen's / policemens')

    Answer: *The policemen's whistles were loud.*

2. The _____ cheese was hard. (mouse's / mouses')

3. Both _____ flags were black. (boat's / boats')

4. The _____ conductor was ready. (choirs' / choir's)

5. _____ friends were coming for tea. (Bess's / Besses')

6. The _____ cake mix was in his bowl. (chef's / chefs')

7. One _____ shoes were missing. (boy's / boys')

8. The _____ supper was ready. (childrens' / children's)

Now try these

Rewrite the following phrases to use the possessive apostrophe rather than the words 'that belong to the'. You will have to rearrange some words. One has been done for you.

1. The manes that belong to the lions

    Answer: *The lions' manes*

2. The sails that belong to the ships

3. The bats that belong to the cricketers

4. The phones that belong to the men

5. The sweets that belong to the children

6. The fields that belong to the farmers

Homophones and near-homophones (I)

Homophones are words that sound the same but they are spelt differently and have different meanings.

Get started

Match each word in the box to the correct meaning. One has been done for you.

accept	except	bury	affect	meddle
	whether	berry	medal	

1. apart from

   Answer: *except*

2. if

3. alter

4. a small juicy fruit

5. agree to

6. interfere

7. put in the ground

8. an award

Try these

Copy out the sentences, choosing the correct word to complete each one. One has been done for you.

1. Serena walked to the front of the hall to _____ her prize. (accept / except)

    Answer: *Serena walked to the front of the hall to <u>accept</u> her prize.*

2. The bird ate the _____ from the bush. (buries / berries)

3. The _____ had started to clear up, so Kamal decided to go out. (whether / weather)

4. Mrs Jones, _____ cat was lost, always hoped he'd return. (whose / who's)

5. Samantha's sister told her not to _____ with her jewellery. (medal / meddle)

6. The recent bad weather _____ the harvest. (affected / effected)

7. The athlete was awarded a gold _____. (medal / meddle)

8. The film had excellent special _____. (affects / effects)

Now try these

Use these words in sentences of your own. An example has been done for you.

except, accept, bury, medal, effect, weather, who's, meddle

Answer: *Taylor disliked all sports <u>except</u> football.*

Homophones and near-homophones (2)

Homophones are words that sound the same but they are spelt differently and have different meanings.

Get started

Match each word in the box to the correct meaning. One has been done for you.

grown	he'll	great	knot	groan
	grate	heal	here	

1. to have become larger

   Answer: *grown*

2. he will

3. shred

4. moan

5. in this place

6. to tie or tangle

7. to make well again

8. really good

Try these

Copy out the sentences, choosing the correct word to complete each one. One has been done for you.

1. Charlie's grandmother said, "You've groan / grown!"

   Answer: *Charlie's grandmother said "You've <u>grown!</u>"*

2. "There are spaces over here / hear," said Julie.

3. If he puts his coat on, heel / he'll feel much warmer.

4. Marek wished he had knot / not eaten all the sweets.

5. Everyone thought the disco was great / grate.

6. The new trainers caused blisters on her heel / heal.

7. At dawn you can hear / here the birds start to sing.

8. I like to great / grate cheese on top of my spaghetti.

Now try these

Use these words in sentences of your own. An example has been done for you.

not, groan, hear, knot, grate, he'll, heal, grown

Answer: *Janet wished she had <u>not</u> left her hat unguarded.*

Homophones and near-homophones (3)

Homophones are words that sound the same but they are spelt differently and have different meanings.

Get started

Match each word in the box to the correct meaning. One has been done for you.

mist	plane	mane	meat	fair
	peace	fare		meet

1. aeroplane

   Answer: *plane*

2. encounter

3. light fog

4. calm, not fighting

5. long fur around an animal's head

6. food made from animals

7. equal or just

8. the cost of a journey

Try these

Copy out the sentences, choosing the correct word to complete each one. One has been done for you.

1. The weather forecast was for _____ on the hills. (mist / missed)

   Answer: *The weather forecast was for __mist__ on the hills.*

2. Jake _____ his friend now that he was gone. (mist / missed)

3. Lucas liked his biscuits _____, without chocolate. (plane / plain)

4. "Would you like a _____ of cake?" asked Peyton. (piece / peace)

5. The _____ meal was to be eaten at 1 p.m. (mane / main)

6. I plan to _____ my friend at 3 p.m., today. (meat / meet)

7. "How much is the bus _____ to town?" (fare / fair)

8. As the last children left, there was _____ again. (piece / peace)

Now try these

Use these words in sentences of your own. An example has been done for you.

mane, mist, plane, peace, meat, fair, fare, plain

Answer: *The lion's __mane__ was long and thick.*

Homophones and near-homophones (4)

Homophones are words that sound the same but they are spelt differently and have different meanings.

Get started

Match each word in the box to the correct meaning. One has been done for you.

bawl	brake	male	seen	reign
	rain	ball		scene

1. to slow down or stop

   Answer: *brake*

2. cry or shout loudly

3. not female

4. looked at

5. rule as king or queen

6. water falling from the sky

7. object used in various sports

8. a section of a play

Try these

Copy out the sentences, choosing the correct word to complete each one. One has been done for you.

1. The burglar had to _____ the window to get in. (brake / break)

   Answer: *The burglar had to <u>break</u> the window to get in.*

2. The tennis _____ crossed the line. (ball / bawl)

3. The old man _____ in his mule. (reined / reigned)

4. The postman delivered my _____ on time this morning. (mail / male)

5. The _____ needed more rehearsal. (scene / seen)

6. Queen Elizabeth II has _____ for over 60 years. (rained / reigned)

7. _____ has fallen in the valleys today. (Rein / Rain / Reign)

8. I have _____ lightning in the sky tonight. (scene / seen)

Now try these

Use these words in sentences of your own. An example has been done for you.

seen, brake, bawl, male, rein, scene, mail, break

Answer: *Sabir had <u>seen</u> the whole match.*

Can you remember the spellings you've learned this term?
Carry out these activities to find out.

A. Correct the spellings of these misspelt words.

1. vaque
2. uneek
3. plage
4. sissors

5. sene
6. gray
7. raindeer
8. mussles

B. Write out these phrases and add the missing apostrophes.

1. the cats ginger coat
2. five minutes peace
3. the ladies bags
4. the horses mane
5. two days extension
6. Jamess parents
7. the bunnies ears
8. this terms goals

C. Copy and complete these sentences by choosing the correct words to fill the gaps.

1. I will not _____ this piece of work. Do it again! (except / accept)

2. I'm afraid your poor spelling will _____ your mark. (affect / effect)

3. The wires for the headphones have got into a terrible _____. (not / knot)

4. Can you pass me the cheese _____, please? (grater / greater)

5. We waited at the corner but we must have _____ you. (missed / mist)

6. The _____ reason I've called you here is to ask a favour. (mane / main)

7. It _____ my heart to see you crying like this. (breaks / brakes)

8. By the time the police arrived at the _____, the pickpocket had vanished. (scene / seen)